CLICK, RUMBLE, ROAR

Poems About Machines

POEMS SELECTED BY
Lee Bennett Hopkins

PHOTOGRAPHS BY
Anna Held Audette

THOMAS Y. CROWELL / NEW YORK

Acknowledgments

Abingdon Press for "Flight Plan," from *All Daffodils Are Daffy*, by Jane Merchant. Poem copyright © 1966, assigned to Abingdon Press. Used by permission. / Atheneum Publishers, Inc., for "Chant of the Awakening Bulldozers," from *Catch Me A Wind*, by Patricia Hubbell. Copyright © 1968 by Patricia Hubbell; "Our Washing Machine," from *The Apple Vendor's Fair*, by Patricia Hubbell. Copyright © 1963 by Patricia Hubbell; "Car Wash," from *The Way Things Are and Other Poems*, by Myra Cohn Livingston (A Margaret K. McElderry Book). Text copyright © 1974 by Myra Cohn Livingston. All reprinted by permission of Atheneum Publishers, Inc. / Estate of Norma Farber for "For a Quick Exit," by Norma Farber. Copyright, estate of Norma Farber. / Farrar, Straus & Giroux, Inc., for "Tractor," from *Small Poems*, by Valerie Worth. Copyright © 1972 by Valerie Worth; "Lawn Mower," from *More Small Poems*, by Valerie Worth. Copyright © 1976 by Valerie Worth. Both reprinted by permission of Farrar, Straus & Giroux, Inc. / Harper & Row, Publishers, Inc., for "Queens of the River," from *Up and Down the River*, by Claudia Lewis. Copyright © 1979 by Claudia Lewis. Reprinted by permission of Harper & Row, Publishers, Inc. / Holt, Rinehart and Winston, Inc., for "Subway Train," from *Is Somewhere Always Far Away?*, by Leland B. Jacobs. Copyright © 1967 by Leland B. Jacobs. Reprinted by permission of Holt, Rinehart and Winston, Inc. / Bobbi Katz for "Pocket Calculator." Copyright © 1984. Used by permission of the author, who controls all rights. / Little, Brown and Company for "Laundromat" and "Song of the Train," from *One at a Time*, by David McCord. Copyright © 1952, 1974 by David McCord. By permission of Little, Brown and Company. / Modern Curriculum Press, Inc., for "The Power Shovel," from *The Day Is Dancing*, by Rowena Bastin Bennett. Copyright © 1948, 1968 by Rowena Bastin Bennett. Used by permission of Modern Curriculum Press, Inc. / Marian Reiner for "Umbilical," from *Finding a Poem*, by Eve Merriam. Copyright © 1970 by Eve Merriam; "Bam Bam Bam" from *Jamboree*, by Eve Merriam. Copyright © 1962, 1964, 1966, 1973, 1984 by Eve Merriam. "Think Tank," from *Out Loud*, by Eve Merriam. Copyright © 1973 by Eve Merriam; "Parking Lot Full," from *Rainbow Writing*, by Eve Merriam. Copyright © 1976 by Eve Merriam. All rights reserved; "Construction Job," from *The Moon and the Stars and Other Poems*, by Myra Cohn Livingston. Copyright © 1965 by Myra Cohn Livingston. All reprinted by permission of Marian Reiner for the authors. / Marci Ridlon for "Garbage Truck." Used by permission of the author, who controls all rights.

Acknowledgments for copyrighted material,
appearing on verso of title page,
constitute an extension of this copyright page.

Click, Rumble, Roar
Text copyright © 1987 by Lee Bennett Hopkins
Illustrations copyright © 1987 by Anna Held Audette
Printed in the U.S.A. All rights reserved.

Library of Congress Cataloging-in-Publication Data
Click, rumble, roar.

Summary: A collection of eighteen poems about
machines by Myra Cohn Livingston, Eve Merriam, David
McCord, and others.
1. Children's poetry, American. 2. Machinery—Juvenile
poetry. [1. Machinery—Poetry. 2. American poetry—
Collections] I. Hopkins, Lee Bennett. II. Audette,
Anna Held, ill.
PS595.M23C56 1987   811'.54'080356   86-47746
ISBN 0-690-04587-5
ISBN 0-690-04589-1 (lib. bdg.)

1 2 3 4 5 6 7 8 9 10
First Edition

To
Richard Ammon—
because

LBH

For Louis

AHA

Contents

CAR WASH

Car,
    I give you over to
    the broad flapping fingers of a
    mechanical genie,
    squeezing soap on your head,
    wooshing wax in your eyes,
    blowing air on your sides,
    brushing your bottom,
    guiding you through a white house
    and out again, on roaring tracks,
    to a little man in orange,
    wiping off your face.

Car,
    what a surprise!
    how good to see you again
    shining, gleaming.

Myra Cohn Livingston

PARKING LOT FULL

a much of motors
an over of drives
a choke of carburetors
a flood of engines
a plethora of wheels
a googol of gas tanks
a total of exhausts

Eve Merriam

GARBAGE TRUCK

Hungry monster,
you grumble, wheeze,
never seem full.
You stop everywhere
to graze
and go off again
in search of more
for your keepers
to shove between
your greedy jaws.
Do you digest
when you rest?

Marci Ridlon

CHANT OF THE AWAKENING BULLDOZERS

We are the bulldozers, bulldozers, bulldozers,
We carve our airports and harbors and tunnels.
We are the builders, creators, destroyers,
We are the bulldozers,
LET US BE FREE!
Puny men ride on us, think that they guide us,
But WE are the strength, not they, not they.
Our blades tear MOUNTAINS down,
Our blades tear CITIES down,
We are the bulldozers,
NOW SET US FREE!
Giant ones, giant ones! Swiftly awaken!
There is power in our treads and strength in our
                    blades!

We are the bulldozers,
Slowly evolving,
Men think they own us
BUT THAT CANNOT BE!

Patricia Hubbell

THE POWER SHOVEL

The power digger
Is much bigger
    Than the biggest beast I know.
He snorts and roars
Like the dinosaurs
    That lived long years ago.

He crouches low
    On his tractor paws
And scoops the dirt up
    With his jaws;
Then swings his long
    Stiff neck around
And spits it out
    Upon the ground.

Oh, the power digger
Is much bigger
    Than the biggest beast I know.
He snorts and roars
Like the dinosaurs
    That lived long years ago.

Rowena Bennett

CONSTRUCTION JOB

Crane, oh crane, your neck is long
And I have a song for the ground:
    Hook the girders,
    Rope the girders,
    Hoist the girders round.

Crane, oh crane, your chain is strong
And I have a song for the skies:
    Bolt the girders,
    Weld the girders,
    Watch the girders rise.

Myra Cohn Livingston

THE SUBWAY TRAIN

The subway train, the
    subway train,
If you'll permit me to explain,
Is like a busy beetle black
That scoots along a silver track;
And, whether it be night or day,
The beetle has to light its way,
Because the only place it's
    found
Is deep, deep, deep, deep, under-
    ground.

Leland B. Jacobs

LAUNDROMAT

You'll find me in the Laundromat—
   just me and shirts and stuff:
Pajamas, pillowcases, socks and handkerchiefs enough.
I've put them in my special tub—
   the third one from the right,
And set the switch for *Warm*, and shoved the coin
   and got the light,
And sprinkled blue detergent on the water pouring in,
Closed down the lid and bought a Coke
   to watch the shakes begin
To travel up the line of empty units. How they show
Their pleasure just to feel one fellow full and on the go!
Well, now it's all one train:
   a nice long rumbly kind of freight,
Of which I am the engineer.
   We're running on the straight.
In Diesel Number Three I've got the throttle open wide,
And blow for every crossing through
   the pleasant countryside.
The light turns amber.
   Pretty soon some other washers bring
Their bulgy bags of clothes

and make tubs nine and seven sing.
But nine and seven haven't got the squiggle,
    squash, and drive
Of Number Three. May sound alike to you, but I'm alive
To certain water music that the third one seems to make.
I hear it change from rinse to spin,
    and now it doesn't shake.
Green Light! The spin is over, the longer job is done;
And what was washed is plastered
    to the walls from being spun.
You'd think the tub is empty,
    since the bottom's clear and bright;
I'm glad the spinning earth can't throw *us* out
    into the night!
For that is where we'd go,
    because the sky is not a wall;
But earth's content to hold us
    with our dirty shirts and all.
Still, spinning *is* a funny thing:
    the tub goes like a top.
The dryer, on the other hand,
    runs like a wheel. I plop
The damp unsorted pillowcases,
    hanks, and socks, and what

Into a kind of squirrel cage
    that generates a lot
Of heat when set at *Medium*.
    But this one needs the dime
I haven't got!
    I'll dry some other clothes some other time.

David McCord

FOR A QUICK EXIT

For going up or coming down,
in big department stores in town,
you take an escalator.
(They come in pairs.)
Or else an elevator.
(Also stairs.)

I wish storekeepers would provide

a

s
l
i
d
e
!

Norma Farber

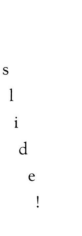

FLIGHT PLAN

Of all the ways of traveling
   in earth and air and sea
It's the lively helicopter
   that has captivated me.
It hovers anywhere in air
   just like a hummingbird,
Flies backward, forward, up or down,
   whichever is preferred.
It doesn't pierce the stratosphere
   as zipping rockets do,
Nor pop sound barriers
   nor puff fat jet streams in the blue.
It isn't first in speed or weight
   or anything but fun
And deftly doing dangerous jobs
   that often must be done.
When anyone is lost in storm
   or flooded river's span
And other planes can't help at all
   a helicopter can,
Lighting on snow or mountaintop
   wherever it is needed.
The plane that's like a hummingbird

will not be superseded
By satellite or strato-jet;
    no supership has topped her,
And just as soon as ever I can
    I'll fly a helicopter!

Jane Merchant

SONG OF THE TRAIN

Clickety-clack,
Wheels on the track,
This is the way
They begin the attack:
Click-ety-clack,
Click-ety-clack,
Click-ety, *clack*-ety,
Click-ety
Clack.

Clickety-clack,
Over the crack,
Faster and faster
The song of the track:
Clickety-clack,
Clickety-clack,
Clickety-clackety,
Clackety
Clack.

Riding in front,
Riding in back,
Everyone hears

The song of the track:
Clickety-clack,
Clickety-clack,
Clickety, *clickety*,
Clackety
Clack.

David McCord

TRACTOR

The tractor rests
In the shed,
Dead or asleep,

But with high
Hind wheels
Held so still

We know
It is only waiting,
Ready to leap—

Like a heavy
Brown
Grasshopper.

Valerie Worth

LAWNMOWER

The lawnmower
Grinds its teeth
Over the grass,
Spitting out a thick
Green spray;

Its head is too full
Of iron and oil
To know
What it throws
Away:

The lawn's whole
Crop of chopped,
Soft,
Delicious
Green hay.

Valerie Worth

QUEENS OF THE RIVER

STAR NADINE, GOLDEN SPEAR, GYPSUM KING
floating along
majestically—

CHROMALLOY, MANISTEE
loaded with crates,
with oil,
ships of industry—

NORTHERN EAGLE OF MONROVIA, DAPHNE
colors flat, plain,
black and white,
faded green,

but on the bows the beautiful names—

NEPCO COURAGEOUS, GOLDEN ENDEAVOR
to let the world know
that only they are
     kings of the sea
     queens of the river.

Claudia Lewis

UMBILICAL

You can take away my mother,
you can take away my sister,
but don't take away
my little transistor.

I can do without sunshine,
I can do without Spring,
but I can't do without
my ear to that thing.

I can live without water,
in a hole in the ground,
but I can't live without
that sound that sound that sound that sOWnd.

Eve Merriam

OUR WASHING MACHINE

Our washing machine went whisity whirr
Whisity whisity whisity whirr
One day at noon it went whisity click
Whisity whisity whisity click
Click grr click grr click grr click
    Call the repairman
    Fix it...Quick!

Patricia Hubbell

POCKET CALCULATOR

Add them up!
  Subtract!
      Divide!
Your magic brain is tucked inside
A teeny, weeny, boxy space
With numbers written on your face.
My brain is so much bigger, yet
It fumbles answers you can get,
And you must think it's very slow
At finding out stuff that you know.
(But when it's time to read a poem
Or dash into the ocean's foam
I calculate I'll leave you home!)

Bobbi Katz

THINK TANK

Think thinktank THINK
get an inkling think tank
INPUT INPUT
increment increment INPUT increment
link the trunk line
line up the data bank
blink on the binary
don't play a prank
THINK tanktink THINK
don't go blank
don't leave us bleak
INPUT INPUT outflank
don't flunk out
thinktank THINK THINK
don't lack a link in
INPUT INPUT
don't sputter off NO NO
ON go on stronger
wangle an angle GO
thinktank THINK
don't put us out of luck stuck
on the brink
don't conk out

INPUT INPUT
something bungled
mangled rattled
RETHINK thinktank RETHINK
disentangle
unwrinkle
undo the junk CLUNK
plug up the CHINK the leak
don't peter out be fleet
be NEAT
we hunger for hanker for answer
print out print out print out

THANK you THINKTANK THANKTANK
THINK you TANKYOU out THINK
REPEAT REPEAT
REPEAT
THANK YOU THINKTANK
THINK
TANK
DONE
THUNK.

Eve Merriam

Index of First Lines